Learn to Swim

The Australian Swim Schools Association is delighted to endorse this book. This is an essential addition to the resources available to parents who wish to establish their precious youngsters on the pathway to a lifetime of fun, health, and safety. Appropriate swimming and water safety lessons for babies and toddlers have many wonderful benefits, significantly enhancing intellectual, physical, social, and emotional development. And it may even save their life!

It is vital that parents can access the creditable, expert insights in Learn to Swim to make the best informed decisions for successful, developmentally appropriate lessons.

**Ross Gage**
**CEO, Australian Swim Schools Association**
**United States Swim Schools Association Hall of Fame**

# Learn to Swim

## Helping Parents Teach Their BABY to Swim

Newborn to 3 Years

Tracey Ayton | Ben Holden

Meyer & Meyer Sport

British Library Cataloguing in Publication Data
A catalogue record for this book is available from the British Library

**Learn to Swim**
Maidenhead: Meyer & Meyer Sport (UK) Ltd., 2019
ISBN 978-1-78255-160-7

© 2019 by Meyer & Meyer Sport (UK) Ltd.
Aachen, Auckland, Beirut, Dubai, Hägendorf, Hong Kong, Indianapolis, Cairo, Cape Town,
Manila, New Delhi, Singapore, Sydney, Tehran, Vienna

Member of the World Sport Publishers' Association (WSPA)
www.w-s-p-a.org

Printed by Print Consult GmbH, Munich, Germany

ISBN: 978255-160-7
E-Mail: i    m-sports.com
www.m-m-    com

# CONTENTS

# INTRODUCTION

We wrote this book so that you, as a parent, will better understand what occurs in baby swimming lessons and how to teach your baby the basics of swimming. In it, we bring our many years of experience in infant swimming, both as teachers and parents and as experts within the Learn to Swim industry.

Sometimes it is what we don't know that can hinder a baby's progress to becoming happy and confident in the water and to enjoy swimming. This book has been designed to help all parents— irrespective of swimming experience—to teach their babies the basics of baby swimming with a step-by-step guide, handy hints, and troubleshooting pointers.

We don't all start our swimming adventures at the same time, and there shouldn't be any comparisons made between children. The most important step is to commit to giving your baby every chance of survival in the water with regular swimming experiences conducted in a safe environment. We recommend swimming with your baby up to twice a week all year round in an indoor heated pool. If the summer time is the only opportunity to swim, then grab it with both hands and swim! The more time in the water you spend with your baby, the faster they learn and retain the skills and the quicker they learn more advanced swimming skills.

We hope you enjoy this book and find the instructions clear and concise. If you get stuck on a particular skill, take a minute, keep your body language relaxed, and try again, or you can try something different and work up to it.

# 1

## BATH TIME

# 1 BATH TIME

The moment your baby has his or her first bath, the relationship with water continues. As babies have spent months in the water of a mother's womb, it is a natural environment for them; newborn babies relax in the bath because it replicates the sensation of being in the womb. Whether the baby is held in a shallow bath or deep bath with perhaps a parent, the water should be a tool to relax and calm the baby. The bath is also an excellent opportunity to educate babies and toddlers in all aspects of swimming and can help reinforce the 'important trigger words and skills learned in lessons.

A warm washcloth placed over the baby's body will provide some added pressure and may help calm the baby if he is a little unsettled (figure 1). For the baby to be relaxed in the bath, it is imperative for the parent to be relaxed as well. The parent must be calm and continue to hold the baby gently and softly, not squeezing as this may alarm the baby and also diminish the experience of floating in the water (figure 2). Think of the water as holding the baby and your hands are only a support.

You can also start the experience of cueing breath control in the bath by gently pouring water over the baby while repeating the cue words: "[Baby's name]...1, 2, 3...Go" or "[Baby's name]...Ready, Go" (figure 3). It doesn't really matter what the words are so long as they are consistent with the water going over baby. You can begin to gently pour water over babies' heads and faces from day one. In fact, it is better to begin this early on rather than wait until they are toddlers.

# Tips for Bath Time

- **No distractions.** Phones should be off or on silent.

- **Prepare** the area with all that you need, including dry towels and a non-slip floor mat.

- **Keep** a flat area outside of the bath for the baby to lie on, if needed.

- **Make sure** all other siblings are supervised and taps are turned off.

- **Do not** leave babies unattended in the bath, even if a bath chair is used.

- **Do not** leave babies in the care of young children.

*Figure 1 Placing a washcloth over the body can help relax an unsettled baby.*

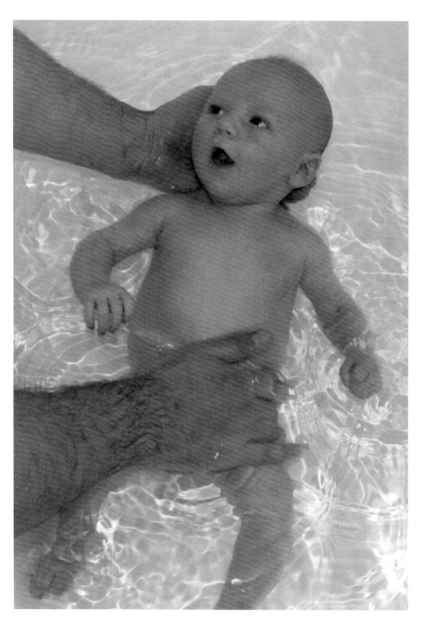

*Figure 2 Soft hands begin in the bath*

Figure 3 "[Baby's name]...

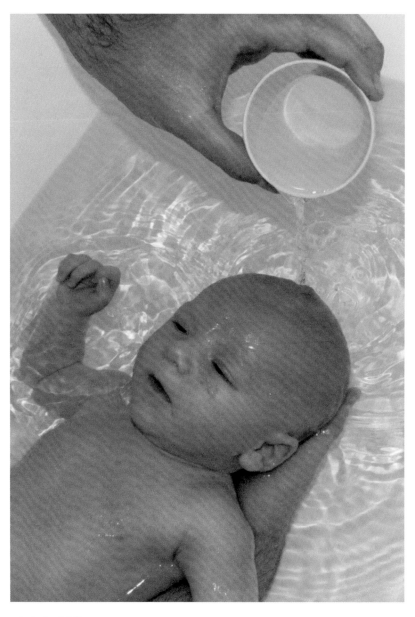

*...1, 2, 3...GO!"*

# 2

# FROM BATH TO POOL

# 2   FROM BATH TO POOL

There are several different ways to progress your baby from the bath to the pool. The easiest way to introduce your baby to the pool is in an informal setting at a local pool with one or both parents in the water. Lots of playing and encouragement helps to alleviate any anxiety a baby may have and create a positive play experience. This positive reinforcement is crucial to future water experiences. The first few trips to the pool give you, the parent, a chance to practice soft hands and maintain a relaxed body, exactly what you practiced in the bath.

The more structured approach will be to join in swimming lessons straight away. The teacher will assist you with holds and the other basics of baby swimming that are outlined in this book. We support a combination of lessons and family fun trips to the pool to fast track your baby's progress in the water.

Ideally, babies will start formal lessons at four to six months. At this age, the baby has sufficient head control to benefit from some of the activities carried out in lessons and to enjoy the experience of being with other babies. It is also important for parents and carers to feel included in an activity with other parents or carers. Often coming to swimming lessons at a young age forms long-time friendships and associations as the children grow. This book covers babies up to 3 years of age, also examining what to expect if they start swimming at a later age. There is no golden rule as to when babies should start swimming, but research shows that the sooner they start, the better the result will be.

If a baby is experiencing floating and water familiarization at home in the bath, she will be prepared when this is replicated in the pool. So, too, will the parents as they are already familiar with the activities and being in the water.

Remember there should be no stress or trauma involved in the baby's swimming. Because babies tend to have their own agendas, there can be a different experience from week to week, so it is very important that everyone remain relaxed.

Did you know that a disposable diaper is often not a swim diaper? If a baby enters the water in a normal disposable diaper, it will swell quite quickly. It can even pop, and the inside gel is very hard to remove from the pool. A swim diaper, however, does not swell, and often it is recommended to wear a reusable diaper or swimming costume over the top of the swim diaper. There are many types of reusable diapers on the market, and some swimming programs are particular about what should be worn. Babies can wear a t-shirt or even a little wetsuit if the pool is cooler, and they feel the cold. Whenever possible, it is best for the baby to wear less clothing so that skin-to-skin contact is established for a relaxed and calm baby.

Adequate clothing for after the class and a head covering if the weather is cool will help baby feel warm and snug. Using pacifiers in the pool is not recommended.

These same recommendations apply if you have chosen to have your lessons in a home pool. If swimming outdoors, you may need to consider sunscreen.

Goggles are not recommended at this age; it is best if the baby experiences the world under the water with eyes wide open!

## How should I prepare for the first swimming lesson?

If you have chosen to enroll in a baby swimming class, you need to think of you and your baby's needs when choosing the day and time. Try to book a timeslot that is not when your baby wants to sleep or feed. Tired and hungry babies are cranky babies.

Between four months and two years, it is generally recommended that a parent or carer take the class with the baby, especially with babies new to the pool. Generally, only one parent or carer should participate in the lesson, and, if possible, that the same parent or carer should come every week. As discussed previously, any tension or stress the parent has in their hands and body will be transfer to the baby, and the baby will also feel stressed or tense. For this reason, try to be consistent with who is in the pool and also make sure it is not a time when the parent is tired or rushed. If the person in the pool needs to change for some reason, just be aware that the baby may respond differently with each individual. On weekends, you will often see lots of Baby and Dad classes, and this is a great time for dads to bond with their babies.

## What do I need to bring with me?

You need to bring a happy, smiling, positive attitude! And also diapers. The diaper policy is different for each pool. Some children don't wear any! If there is accident in the pool, or a Code Brown as it is known, the pool could be closed. For this reason, a swim diaper is usually recommended. A swim diaper is specifically designed for the pool and essential to maintain pool water quality and hygiene.

# 3  BABY SWIMMING LESSON ESSENTIALS

## What do I look for in a baby swimming program?

There are many different swim programs available for babies all over the world. It is a good idea to do some research on the program that you are thinking of joining. You should carefully check things like water temperature, cleanliness of the center and changing rooms, access, number of children in the class, and what makes up the baby program. Some baby programs are based on play and singing songs, and the same class is taught each week. The more advanced baby swimming classes teach a progressive submersion-based program in which new skills are introduced each week. Skill-based learning progressions mean your baby can advance to a higher level when they are ready to progress. All baby swimming programs should be positive, and they should never use force, create trauma for the baby, or force separation from the parent.

Once you have identified a possible program that suits your needs, visit and observe the classes held there. Ideally, babies grouped by age and similar motor skills in a class is preferable. A place that makes you feel comfortable and relaxed is also important. Often you can tell a good center by the support and knowledge of the staff when signing up.

# 3

# BABY SWIMMING
# LESSON ESSENTIALS

## What can I expect to happen when I attend lessons?

Remember to research the center prior to your first lesson. Check out parking and access. Is there room to store strollers, or is it best to carry your baby in. Make sure to give yourself plenty of time to get to the lesson in a relaxed fashion and not be rushed. A 20-minute relaxed lesson is better than a 30-minute one if you are stressed.

Once at the lesson, you should be introduced to your teacher and other classmates. Use your teacher's name often to your baby and in return use your baby's name often when in the class. This will help the baby feel more comfortable with the teacher and in return will help the teacher remember each baby. Most likely the center's diaper policy will be checked with each participant, and there will be an introduction about the goal of the class and what is expected from all involved.

Often there is a song that will commence the class, letting parents and swimmers know that the class has begun.

# 4

# HOLDING THE BABY
# AND BODY LANGUAGE

# 4 HOLDING THE BABY AND BODY LANGUAGE

## How to hold and support your baby in the water

There are many different ways that you can hold your baby in the water. Swim schools will have preferred holds that they use. The main thing to remember is that the water holds your baby, and you are the additional support around this. The most important tool that you can bring into the pool with your baby are your hands. Any anxiety or stress that you may feel in the pool will transfer directly through your hands to your baby, so remember to stay calm and relaxed while gently holding your baby.

It is best for you and your baby to be at the same height in the pool, usually at the point where the water meets the air. For you and your baby to be at this level, you will most likely need to bend your knees slightly. Make sure that both of your feet are firmly planted on the bottom of the pool and push your backside out like you are sitting on a chair. This will ensure that you do not slip, are able to move quickly if needed, and you protect your back.

Keep your hands soft and light. If you grip or squeeze the baby too tightly, it will reinforce to the baby that this is a negative situation. Your body language needs to be positive, relaxed, and happy, including lots of eye contact, positive facial expressions, and verbal encouragement. Following are a few holds that we have found effective over the years of teaching. They can be used with babies of any age and ability.

## FACE-TO-FACE HOLD

The face-to-face hold (figure 4) creates direct eye contact between you and your baby, which is particularly great for beginners in the pool.

Place your hands under the baby's chest with your thumbs up around each shoulder. Think of your hands as a little platform for your baby to lie on while they feel their own buoyancy in the water. The thumbs are up on the shoulders to assist with your hold, but do not squeeze or apply too much pressure. The baby is balancing in your hands in the water.

Maintain a relaxed, low body position so you remain eye-to-eye with your baby. Your shoulders should also be low in the water and your arms outstretched in front of you. If you are feeling the weight of the baby in your shoulders, you are too high in the water. Check again that your hands are facing up, gently supporting the baby's body, and thumbs remain relaxed.

*Figure 4 Face-to-face hold*

While walking backwards with your baby (figure 5), gently sway him from side to side in a seaweed-like motion so he relaxes and unwinds. Lots of positive facial expressions, blowing bubbles, soft talking, and songs will enhance this experience.

*Figure 5 Walking backwards using the face-to-face hold*

## TORSO HOLD

Gently hold the baby around the torso below the armpits so you are both facing the same direction (figure 6). The torso hold is easy to do and a great introduction to the sandwich hold or chasing after floating toys in the water. You can easily move and gently swish around the pool.

*Figure 6 Torso hold*

## UPRIGHT HOLD

To use the upright hold (figure 7), face the baby away from you and hold him up against your chest. Place one hand under the baby's bottom for support while using your other hand to support the baby's chest, arm, or leg.

*Figure 7 Upright hold*

## SANDWICH HOLD

Start the sandwich hold (figure 8) with your baby by your side, keeping low in the water.

Place one hand under the baby's torso and the other along the top of the baby's back. Keep the hold light so the baby can feel his balance in the water and start to make his own adjustments when needed. From here, step forward and glide the baby along the surface of the water like a boat. Scattering a few toys around the pool to collect and move around the water makes this a fun game. One of the big advantages of this hold is that the baby's arms and legs can interact freely with the water, making submersions (covered in a later chapter) super easy.

*Figure 8 Sandwich hold*

# 5

# BREATH CONTROL
# AND CUEING

# 5    BREATH CONTROL AND CUEING

You can begin breath control and cueing at home in the bath when your baby is four months old. Cueing is the verbal instruction that tells the baby that water will be coming over their face and prepares them to swim underwater.

Common cues are "1, 2, 3" or "Ready, Go." The cue can be anything, in any language, so long as it is consistent and begins with the baby's name.

For those not practicing this activity at home, it will be introduced in the swimming class. Usually the instructor will take a cup of water and gently pour it in front of the baby, then possibly over the baby's hands and body so that she can see and feel the flow of the water. Then the cue will be given, and the water gently poured over the baby's head so that it goes down her face.

A young baby has an innate reflex that causes her to close her eyes and hold her breath as the water passes over her face. By repeating the cue with this activity, the baby will learn to do this prior to the water coming over her face and not when the water goes over the face. The parent should be able to see this process develop and understand what it means. Older babies who have outgrown the automatic shutdown reflex will take longer to learn this action. Some may protest at the activity, and it is important to always be positive and not persist it if the baby is too stressed.

Older babies not having their hair and face washed at home because of a dislike of water on their face will find cueing and breath control a little harder to establish, but it should not be ignored.

## STEP 1

Initially you can establish the cueing process by pouring water over the legs and body. Make sure baby is relaxed and calm before starting. The key is to keep the words and timing consistent. In figures 9 and 10, Baby Mason is sitting on a mat, calm and relaxed. The parent then begins the cueing.

*Figure 9 The cues: "Mason..." [pause] "Ready..." [pause] "Go!"*

*Figure 10 After the cues, water is gently poured over Mason's arms and legs.*

## STEP 2

Start in the same position as in the beginner process. Cue the exact same way, beginning with the baby's name, and pour water over the baby's head and face in a smooth action. The baby is now establishing breath control as the water goes over his face. Repeat this step using the cue and watch for signs of breath control. When the baby exhibits breath control, he closes his eyes and holds his breath. The baby will then learn to control his breath whenever the cue is used.

*Figure 11 "Mason..." [pause] "Ready..." [pause] "Go!" Then gently pour the water over the baby's head.*

# 6

# FLOATING ON
# THE BACK

# 6    FLOATING ON THE BACK

Floating on the back can be one of the most difficult skills to teach a child to do at a later age, so starting this exercise early is the key to learning this skill. At an early age, a baby can and should be floating on the back during bath time. It is okay if the baby gets water in his ears. Until the baby can sit up, floating on the back should be an easy skill to master.

## BEGINNER

Gently place one hand under your baby's back and let the other rest lightly on the chest (figure 12). The baby's head can rest against your chest as you look down at him. A young baby's head is the heaviest part of the body and may need to be supported at first.

You can try place the baby's head on your shoulder, if needed, but in this case the baby's head is supported on your shoulder, and there is no feeling of buoyancy. If the head is just docked against your chest, the baby can experience the head floating along with the rest of the body (figure 13).

*Figure 12 Beginner back float*

*Figure 13 Beginner back float using the parent's shoulder to support the baby's head*

## INTERMEDIATE

Remove your top hand when you feel comfortable and position the baby away from your body at arms' length (figure 14).

*Figure 14 Intermediate back float, positioning the baby's body away from parent*

## ADVANCED

Remove your bottom hand, completely allowing the baby to float independently. This is fantastic progress! Do not rush through this step as independent floating takes time. Remember to progress through the steps presented in this book, and do not push your baby to do any type of swimming that may make her uncomfortable.

# Troubleshooting

As the baby gets older, the urge to sit upright will overcome the wish to lie on the back in the water. There are several different strategies that you can use in this instance to get the baby to be happy on his back again. Distracting your baby with a toy or a mirror is an ideal way to keep him happy while he is floating on his back (figure 15). Also, singing under the water or blowing bubbles can also keep your baby happy because he hears and feels the vibrations under the water. Never force your baby to stay in a back float position if they are unhappy. Softly massaging the baby's back while in a back float can also help him to relax.

Often a baby's legs will go up in the air when in a back float due to an innate reflex at this stage of development. By sea-weeding back and forth while in the back float position, your baby will lower and relax his legs.

*Figure 15 Using a toy or a mirror can help distract an unsettled baby.*

# 7

## KICKING

# 7    KICKING

At a younger age, a baby's kick is initiated by a reflex action until the brain develops and begins to understand what kicking is. Babies will move their legs backwards and forwards in the water, or sometimes they will not move their legs at all and just glide.

Once they develop the process behind the kicking action or the instruction of kicking, they will move their legs to kick up and down or continue with their backward and forward movement like a breaststroke kick motion, often referred to as splashy toes or pushy toes. At this stage of development, there really should be no stress as to what type of kick is occurring, but rather joy that something is being initiated by the child.

## BEGINNER

Hold the baby in the upright hold (see figure 7) just on the surface of the water and encourage lots of kicking and splashing (figure 16).

*Figure 16 Beginner kicking*

## INTERMEDIATE

Support the baby with the face-to-face hold (see figure 4) and walk slowly backwards in the water while saying, "Kick, kick, kick, kick!" (figure 17).

*Figure 17 Intermediate kicking*

# MOVING THE ARMS

# 8 MOVING THE ARMS

Arm movement may occur naturally as the baby seeks to find her way through the water. Manipulated arm movement may be introduced by the teacher or parent but does not really develop for the baby until around age two. The arm movement should be a reach and pull of the arms under the water. The baby learns to *feel* the water with her hands and moves the water in a digging motion that propels her forward.

Beginning around 18 months, kicking and independent arm movement can be introduced. This can initially be practiced with the head and chest above the water while the parent holds the baby in the upright hold and then progresses to the torso hold. For babies from four months to two years, it is recommended that movement be as natural and relaxed as possible.

## BEGINNER

Hold the baby in the upright hold (see figure 7) just on the surface of the water and encourage lots of arms splashing (figure 18).

*Figure 18 Beginner arm splashing*

## INTERMEDIATE

Support the baby under the chest using the torso hold and gently move one of the hands in a paddling motion to establish the correct paddling movement (figure 19). Using verbal instructions such as "Paddle! Paddle!" while the baby independently moves his arms can also help the baby develop this skill faster. At this stage of development, the baby should be encouraged to dig in the water to get a sense of how it feels to reach and pull while swimming. After age three, the baby is not encouraged to splash at the water but rather to gain more of an understanding for what is happening with the hands under the water, but at this point, the baby need only feel the movement.

*Figure 19 Intermediate arms—paddling while supporting under the chest. Encourage your baby with verbal instructions, such as, "Paddle, Paddle!"*

# 9

# GOING UNDERWATER

# 9    GOING UNDERWATER

By this point, you should have practiced good breath control with your baby, and it is time to put this practice into the activity of submersion. You will use the cueing process to gently put your baby under the water and then bring him to the surface, softly and with a lot of positive language, smiling, and verbal encouragement. Try to keep the level of enthusiasm soft and not too noisy and disruptive to the process. Many parents tend to scream to the rooftops after a submersion, which can startle the baby!

All babies are different, and not all will be ready at the same stage as everyone else in the class. There should be no pressure on the parent to submerge their baby.

We will go through the progressions for submersion starting with the face-to-face hold and finishing with an independent swim.

Remember that with submersions it is best to make the submersion complete with all of the baby's head and body under the surface of the water. You do not have to submerge the baby too deep at first. Often parents think it is kind just to do half of a submersion for their baby, when actually this confuses the baby's brain and cueing process; the baby does not know if he is up above the water and should breathe or down under the water and should initiate breath control. Using what we have already learned, begin with the face-to-face hold, cueing your baby and watching for the signs of breath control. The signs include closing the eyes and holding the breath. Before submersing the baby, say, "[Baby's name]...1 2, 3... Go!" and gently lower the baby completely under the water and then up to you for a big smile and hug! If you feel unsure that your baby is ready for this step or if there are no signs of breath control, stop and go back to practicing pouring a cup of water over the baby's head while saying the cue words (chapter 5).

## BEGINNER

Hold the baby in the face-to-face position (see figure 4). Position at the same height as your baby so both of your heads are just above the water. Begin your cue and watch for signs of breath control (figure 20a) and then lower your baby completely under the water (figure 20b). Slowly bring your baby toward you (figure 20c), and then raise your baby up above the water, being sure to praise them! (figure 20d). Keep the speed of lowering and lifting consistent and steady.

*Figure 20a Hold your baby in the face-to-face position and begin cueing: "Mason..." [pause] "Ready..." [pause] "Go!"*

Figure 20b Lower your baby in the water until he is totally submerged.

Figure 20c Steadily bring your baby toward you (about 2 seconds).

*Figure 20d Raise your baby above the water and cheer, "Well done!"*

## INTERMEDIATE

Begin with the sandwich hold (figure 21). Because you are cheek to cheek with this hold, you can easily say the cue while in this position. Cue your baby and watch for the signs of breath control. The signs include closing the eyes and holding his breath. To begin, say, "[Baby's name]...1, 2, 3... Go!" and then gently lower him under the water and gliding forward one step to gently surface, bring your baby's cheek up to yours.

*Figure 21 Sandwich hold underwater. Hands are placed on either side of the torso with fingers facing forward.*

## ADVANCED

Once your baby has established breath control and is comfortable being submerged under the water, you can release your baby. At this point, the baby will often initiate the movement. In some cases, babies who are very relaxed and savvy under the water will often travel through the water before learning to walk!

Hold your baby facing you and then begin your cueing, watching for those signs of breath control (closing the eyes and holding his breath (figure 22a). Lower your baby under the water (figure 22b), and then let go for three seconds (figure 22c). Count: "1....2....3," and then slowly lift the baby up, praising them for doing such a good job (figure 22d). You've done it! The first swim!

*Figure 22a Hold your baby in face-to-face position and begin cueing: "Mason..." [pause] "Ready..." [pause] "Go!"*

*Figure 22b Lower your baby in the water until he is totally submerged.*

*Figure 22c Release your baby and take a step back. Count slow to three.*

*Figure 22d Slowly lift your baby above the water and cheer! Well done on the very first swim!*

Often parents think their baby needs a little assistance with his or her underwater journey and tend to pull the baby toward them too hard or push the baby forward with too much force. This is really unpleasant for the baby as excessive force will result with water going up the baby's nose and down the windpipe. Think of the submersion as a soft experience of underwater discovery.

# 10

## PUTTING IT
## ALL TOGETHER

# 10 PUTTING IT ALL TOGETHER

A baby can move various ways in the water. A young baby will move because of several innate reflexes. You often hear parents saying how strong a kicker their baby is as she moves her legs backwards and forwards when placed on her tummy. This is often a reflex action of the baby and not an actual thought pattern in which the baby thinks, "I must kick my legs."

Until a baby establishes the brain development that initiates movement, either the reflex action causes this or the parent manipulates the arms and legs of the child to simulate the movement that is needed.

You can use all the holds in this book with submersion and then add a release. For example, in the face-to-face hold, you can cue, submerge, release the baby, and let her travel forward before taking her in your hands to initiate surfacing for air. As a baby develops, she will initiate her own surfacing, either to a parent or the wall of the pool. The parents should encourage the baby to self-initiate surfacing by offering their arms to the baby or allowing the baby to grab a t-shirt for assistance to surface.

It is very important to think of the release as a gentle experience for the baby to discover movement in the water. If the baby is pushed through the water, he will just experience the push and not identify the need for movement. At first, the baby's movement may just be a glide, but then as he develops, so, too, will more movement of the legs, torso, and then, finally, as an evolving toddler, a reach and pull or digging movement of the arms and hands.

*Figure 23 Sandwich hold and release*

# 11

# TROUBLESHOOTING

# 11 TROUBLESHOOTING

The parent or carer plays a critical part in how much their baby enjoys swimming. In our experience, it is better to treat your baby as a student to maximize the rate of learning.

We have discussed the importance of soft hands and positive body language, facial expressions, and dialogue. Often a parent does not even realize that he or she is possibly creating a negative experience for their child. Check that you are relaxed and your hands are soft, and then go through this troubleshooting chapter.

## Be prepared!

First of all, make sure that you are organized on the day of the lesson and have packed everything you need. Arriving at swim lessons without a swim diaper can be a total waste of a class. Many swim schools will not allow you in the water without a swim diaper, so it's best to be prepared. Make sure that you give yourself plenty of time to arrive on time. Being a rushed, stressed parent will transfer the same energy to any aged baby or toddler. Twenty minutes of a relaxed lesson is more beneficial than 30 minutes of a stressful one, so if you are running late, do not get irritated.

Make sure you are happy and comfortable before, during, and after swimming. Wear clothing that is easy to remove on arrival and bring adequate swimwear for the class. It is not a fashion show; a string bikini top that may become a wardrobe malfunction is not ideal. Be prepared to get wet. Whatever you expect your baby to do, you should be happy to do as well. If getting your hair wet or having your mascara run is a problem, then wear a swim cap and do not wear makeup.

## What to eat and drink before lessons.

It is recommended that you not give your baby fluids or solids for approximately one hour prior to the class, if possible. A full tummy can lead to a full diaper and also possible regurgitation. If this happens, it is regarded as a "contamination" in most pools, and the lessons will stop while the pool is cleaned and dosed appropriately with chemicals to stop any potential threat of disease. This can cause some pools to shut down for the day or certainly a period of several hours. Pacifiers are not normally recommended in pools, but it is up to the discretion of the center, as is breastfeeding.

## Who is in the pool?

If dad is in the pool and mom is poolside with a look of fear, this may lead to a hysterical and unhappy baby. Take turns to bathe your baby and learn the soft hands we refer to in this book. If only the mother bathes the baby, the father might not have the soft hands needed for a relaxed baby during swim lessons.

## Dad's time!

Swimming lessons are a great time for Dad and Baby to bond in the water. In today's working environment, there is often not a lot of time that dads get to spend with their babies due to long working hours and busy schedules. Swimming lessons are a great experience for dad and baby, and an experience we fully support! Remember to focus on what is happening in the water and how your baby is feeling. If mom is also at the pool, there needs to be a lot of positivity from both parents in and out of the water. If the parents switch roles week to week, they should both talk about where the baby is in the lesson. There can be a change in the baby's behavior from one parent to another, and if this is the case, keep the same parent teaching your baby in the short term.

## Upset babies in the pool.

All babies will have good days and bad days in the pool. Their being upset may have nothing to do with being in the pool. They might be teething, tired, going through a growth stage, or getting sick. The most important thing to do is try to settle your baby and not compare him with other babies. All babies progress at different rates, and they have a long way ahead of them to master the skill of swimming. Do not at any time feel pressured to achieve a certain level. If your baby is upset, it is best to take a toy and have some timeout from the class while staying in the pool until he settles. There is not point trying to push babies through activities when they are upset and not up for it. You can always rejoin the class when baby is happy.

## The terrible twos!

As your baby nears the two-year-old mark, she starts to develop her own personalities. Your little baby could suddenly develop a larger-than-life personality of her own, and it may not be the one that you expected. Behavioral management in the pool starts in the home, and strategies that are used to encourage two-year-olds to be compliant are up to each individual and can vary a great deal. Some two-year-olds like to bring a favorite toy to the pool; some work on a reward basis for what is expected of them; and others like to mimic older siblings.

Whatever the case may be, it is best to let your instructor know of any difficulty you may be having with your child and how this could impact their behavior in the pool. It could be that an arrival of a new sibling at home or the start of day care can alter the behavior of a child in the pool.

## Language around the baby as they grow.

As the baby grows into a toddler, he or she will start to understand what is being said around them and pick up on body language both positive and negative. The following statements are often said without fully understanding their meaning and consequences:

My baby doesn't like the water. This is often said while the baby is splashing her hands and kicking her feet in the water. It is usually the parent who does not like the water. The baby is enjoying the experience but will pick up on the parent's body language and respond negatively. There could also be other reasons why the baby is upset (see "Upset babies in the pool.").

My baby doesn't like strangers. This is said when the teacher tries to interact with the baby. The parent may not trust the teacher yet or not want to give the baby to the teacher. Try to be a little more tactful and let the baby interact with the teacher with eye contact or touch.

My baby is not feeling well, so we will not go under the water today. If this is the case, maybe you should be at home and not at the pool! Think about the risk of spreading germs to others if your baby is sick or unwell.

My baby does not like going under the water. This is usually heard from the parent who is fearful of their baby going under the water or not confident of submerging their baby. If your baby is cueing normally and happy to go under the water but perhaps you are not, ask the teacher to help you with this process. This will also help you create a great bond between your baby and the teacher.

## Will my baby drink the water?

If breath control is established, there should be no swallowing of water in the class. Sometimes if a baby is submerged without established breath control, then there could be an intake of water. This is not at all recommended. If you are unsure whether your baby should be going under the water, then do not do it! Signs that your baby may be taking in water are vomiting, diarrhea, extended abdomen, and a lot of crying. Some babies will experiment with the taste of the water and actually seek to sip at it. This should be deterred.

Some babies will go under the water with open mouths. If there is established and initiated breath control, they will not take in water. The water may go into their mouth, but not past their throat, and will expel from the mouth if contained there upon surfacing.

A positive environment is really important for babies to grow in the water. You want to set a soft, caring, nurturing, and exploratory scene for swimming lessons and aquatic play. As your baby grows into the toddler stage, heading toward years two and three, there will be a time when you stay out of the swimming pool during lessons, and the child will be in the care of their swimming teacher. At this stage, it is even more essential for a happy and positive environment to be in place.

For your child to trust in the care of his or her teacher, they must also feel that you have trust in the teacher, too. It is often harder for the parent to leave the class as they feel that this very important time with their child in the water has come to an end. You must have your lottery-winning face on at all times and try to alleviate any anxiety that the child is feeling with this process. Lots of praise, encouragement, and smiling works best.

# 12

## SWIMMING SAFER

# 12 SWIMMING SAFER

You can't guarantee that you will keep a child safe in and around the water. There is always a risk element involved, and that is why we refer to swimming as keeping a child safer in the water. Drowning deaths in children under three are tragically high across the globe, and sadly most of them could have been avoided. For every fatal drowning that is reported there are many more non-fatal drownings that often leave a child with permanent brain damage and a family to cope. Unfortunately, in today's society, there is a real belief of "it won't happen to me" when it comes to drowning incidents. Sadly, it does happen, and this is why it is important to follow the rules of safer swimming. Doing so will ensure that you and your family learn to love and respect the water at all times.

So what can you do to make your child a safer swimmer?

## Supervision

Supervision is the number one key to keeping children safer in the water. There is no substitute for constant, adequate, adult supervision of a child in or around the water. The supervisor needs to be vigilant and within arm's reach of the child. The adult should not be sitting in a chair poolside while the child is in the pool. Make sure that you know who is watching the child, particularly if there are a few running around. If the supervisor changes, make sure this is communicated to everyone in the pool area. Many tragic incidents take place when one parent thought the other was the active supervisor of the child. Children under the age of three also need to be constantly supervised around any body of water. This can include the bath, ponds, wading pools, and even pet bowls and toilets. Many drownings have occurred in all these situations, so they should never be overlooked.

## Barriers

Barriers around the water can include several things. They can be physical barriers like pool fences and gates that will keep wandering toddlers out of the pool area unsupervised. These barriers should always be checked for possible ways that a child could gain entry (the internet is full of examples of clever toddlers sneaking past fences). Barriers can also be specific pool rules. Examples include needing permission to enter the water or no swimming without a swimming costume on. You can think of some specific rules that will make sense with your child. As a child gains confidence in the water, a verbal barrier like "Never swim without an adult" is a simple rule for any child as they grow and want to experiment with independence.

## Swimming skills and floatation aids

Don't fall into the false sense of security that because your child is having swimming lessons they don't need as much supervision. Swimming skills in a young child do not negate adult supervision or the use of a floatation aid. Frequently, swimming professionals see a child taught without floatation aids in the class and then put into flotation aids after lessons and left alone in the pool while a parent sits out of the water. Many drownings and non-fatal drownings occur because the child has returned to the water without their aid, thinking they can achieve the same level of swimming as with it.

Flotation aids can help children to be independent in the water, but they can also come undone, get tangled, or tip over. When using a floatation aid like a baby seat, ensure there is constant adult supervision taking place.

## Emergency planning

If your child is missing around the water, check the water first! Time spent looking under beds rather than in the pool is critical. The more time the brain is without oxygen, the higher the likelihood of damage to the brain.

Learn CPR. Many lives lost could have been saved if CPR had been administrated straight away. This is a vital component in saving lives during a drowning incident, and there are many courses available for you.

If you follow all this advice, you will be a safer swimming family and will help reduce the global drowning epidemic. Become an advocate and pass this message on to your friends and family.

# 13

## BABIES WITH
## SPECIAL NEEDS

# 13  BABIES WITH SPECIAL NEEDS

If your baby has a disability or is diagnosed with special needs of any kind, there is no reason why you and your baby cannot enjoy and benefit from being in the water and participating in swimming lessons. This is a very important time for you to bond with your baby and for you both to fall in love with the water. In some cases, additional support is needed for those babies with weaker head control or those with a lower immune system. Regardless of the disability, we believe that all babies benefit from the effects that being in the water brings. Some babies may benefit more from being in a salt water pool rather than chlorine, and some may need to be in a smaller pool with a reduced number of students rather than a large center.

Author Tracey Ayton is a very experienced infant teacher and a specialist in teaching children with disabilities. She has taught children with down syndrome, global delay, physical deformities, blindness, deafness, and many other chromosomal disorders. The overarching message and one that cannot be reinforced enough is what incredible benefits activities in the water brings to any child with physical or mental disabilities.

In this newborn up to three years age group, the needs of the baby are usually not guided by their disability, so any good infant program should be able to cater to these needs. The baby's health professional can advise on anything specific that may be required. Taking this advice, the parent can ask specific questions regarding the swim program. The specifics, though, in seeking out a swim school once the child has left the baby program will be far more involved and will require additional research.

Just a few of the physical benefits include an enhancement of muscular strength, balance, lung capacity, and coordination. Tracey has found participation in baby classes provides an important social inclusion for both the baby and the parent. As your baby progresses to the toddler and preschool developmental stage, more specific skills and techniques may need to be addressed. Always consult with your health professional and make the step to join in swimming lessons.

# 14

## THE FINAL WORD

# 14 THE FINAL WORD

We hope you have enjoyed reading this book as much as we have enjoyed putting it together! We are passionate baby swimming advocates and have seen first hand the benefits that regular baby swimming classes bring. Our goal is to provide parents with the right tools to enhance and accelerate their baby's happiness in the water without information overload.

We believe all babies can learn, thrive, and survive in the water in a caring environment, paving the way for a life full of surfing, water skiing, boating, and many more fun things we do in and on the water. With drowning incidents in this age group at an all-time high across the globe, we believe the key to help reduce this statistic is by providing key swimming information to parents in a clear and concise fashion that is easy to follow and affordable.

Baby swimming has come along in leaps and bounds over the past 10 years. The days of throwing a child in the deep end to sink or swim are long gone, and for good reason. Every child starts his or her swimming journey at different times and in different circumstances. We know how beneficial it is to start the baby early and what you can teach them. By using the information in this book, you will be well prepared to start your baby on a lifelong swimming journey.

Enjoy your swimming!

*–Tracey Ayton and Ben Holden*

# ABOUT THE AUTHORS

With more than 25 years in the Learn to Swim industry, Tracey Ayton has experience in every role from teacher to trainer, coach to manager, and even therapist. With a focus on drowning prevention, she has developed an award-winning baby program and the current curriculum at Little Heroes Swim Academy, a swim school that specializes in teaching students with disabilities.

Tracey is currently a presenter of the Swim Australia Teacher of Swimming, Infants and Toddlers and Learners with a Disability teacher accreditation courses. She received the Austswim Teacher of the Year for infant and preschool swimming for two consecutive years, the Swim Australia Meritorious Award for outstanding service in the Learn to Swim program, and many other community service awards. She is also a member of the Australian Swim Schools Association Water Safety and Inclusion Committees. A regular conference presenter at state, national, and international levels, Tracey is a highly sought after and respected voice in the Learn to Swim industry.

For the past six years, Tracey has taught children with disabilities. After founding a charity in 2012, she formed Little Heroes Swim Academy. This academy provides aquatic education to children with both physical and intellectual disabilities. In 2018, this charity was recognized by the Australian Swim Schools Association and inducted in the Hall of Fam in the Humanitarian category—a worldwide recognition. The award was also presented at the 2018 International Swim Schools Spectacular Conference.